To

Hazel

From

Mary   Sept 10, 2004

You're the Purrfect Friend!

My Purrfect Friend

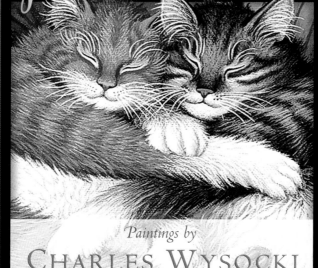

Paintings by
CHARLES WYSOCKI

HARVEST HOUSE PUBLISHERS

EUGENE, OREGON

My Purrfect Friend

Text Copyright © 2004 by Harvest House Publishers
Artwork Copyright © 2004 by Charles Wysocki Inc.
Artwork Copyright © 2004 Mosaic Licensing, Inc.
Published by Harvest House Publishers
Eugene, Oregon 97402

ISBN 0-7369-1360-2

Mosaic Licensing, Inc.
675 Ygnacio Valley Road, Suite B207
Walnut Creek, CA 94596
(925) 934-0889

Design and production by Garborg Design Works, Minneapolis, Minnesota

Harvest House Publishers has made every effort to trace the ownership of all poems and quotes. In the event of a question arising from the use of a poem or quote, we regret any error made and will be pleased to make the necessary correction in future editions of this book.

Printed in Hong Kong

04 05 06 07 08 09 10 11 12 / NG / 10 9 8 7 6 5 4 3 2 1

To gain the friendship of a cat is a difficult thing. The cat is a philosophical, methodical, quiet animal, tenacious of its own habits, fond of order and cleanliness, and it does not lightly confer its friendship. If you are worthy of its affection, a cat will be your friend, but never your slave. He keeps his free will, though he loves, and he will not do for you what he thinks is unreasonable. But if he once gives himself to you it is with absolute confidence and affection.

THEOPHILE GAUTIER

Good friends are good for your health.

IRWIN SARASON

There is, indeed, no single quality of the cat
that man could not emulate to his advantage.

CARL VAN VECHTEN

May you always find your treasure
In the blessings that life sends,
In the beauty of each season,
In the company of friends.

May you grow in faith and wisdom,
Gather strength from every storm...
May you always have a smile to share
And one to keep you warm.

May each path you choose bring promise
Of the things you're dreaming of,
May your world be filled with peace and joy,
Your heart be filled with love.

AUTHOR UNKNOWN

*Animals are
such agreeable
friends, they ask
no questions, they
pass no criticisms.*

GEORGE ELIOT

All cats love a cushioned couch.

THEOCRITUS

*A friend is a
speaking acquaintance
who also listens.*

ARTHUR H. GLASGOW

A friend may well
be reckoned the
masterpiece of nature.

RALPH WALDO EMERSON

You know you're a cat person, even years before you have your first cat, just as some people know they were born to be writers.

LISA ANGOWSKI ROGAK

Why do I like cats?
They're capable of
being very loyal and
forming what passes
for an emotional
attachment without
giving in totally and
losing anything of
themselves. It's a trait
I admire in humans—
something we might
all strive for.

MARCIA MULLER

*A friend is a shoulder to
lean on, an ear to listen,
and a heart to comfort.*

AUTHOR UNKNOWN

*All your wondrous wealth of hair;
Dark and fair,
Silken-shaggy, soft and bright
As the clouds and beams of night...*

ALGERNON CHARLES SWINBURNE

The first duty of love is to listen.

PAUL TILLICH

I have to say that I find a love of cats a very sympathetic quality in people. And conversely, I wonder about people who really dislike cats.

ALICE ADAMS

A best friend is a sister that
destiny forgot to give you.

AUTHOR UNKNOWN

*Friends are notes to life's great
songs, a melody that carries you.*

AUTHOR UNKNOWN

*There is a destiny that makes us brothers,
no one goes his way alone;
all that we send into the lives of others,
comes back into our own.*

EDWIN MARKHAM

My cat has a grounding effect on me. Animals have a kind of fundamental and uncomplicated connectedness to life that people typically don't have and that I like to be reminded of.

MARY GAITSKILL

And we come up with a rationale: they're beautiful, they're intelligent, they're independent. We can go on and on, and it really doesn't get to the heart of it. I couldn't say why I love cats any more than why I love Mozart instead of Mahler. I can't explain why we fall in love with someone. That's just the way it is.

LLOYD ALEXANDER

A cheerful friend is like a sunny

day spreading brightness all around.

JOHN LUBCOCK

13

*Somehow, cats, flowers, houseplants, and Turkish
rugs all seem to go together, the house seems
incomplete with any one of them missing.*

JOHN CASEY

*A friend is someone who reaches
for your hand and touches your heart.*

KATHLEEN GROVE

Cats are beautiful. Siamese, especially, are like living sculpture.
They're mysterious; they jog my imagination. They're very
independent, and I admire that, being rather independent myself.
They're unpredictable, which makes them constantly interesting.
They're intelligent, more so than humans sometimes think.

LILIAN JACKSON BRAUN

God wills that we have sorrows here,
And we will share it;
Whisper thy sorrow in my ear,
That I may also bear it.
If anywhere our trouble seems
To find an end,
'Tis in the fairy land of dreams,
Or with a friend.

ALFRED, LORD TENNYSON

Friends are angels
following you through life.

AUTHOR UNKNOWN

If we would build on a sure foundation in friendship, we must love friends for their sake rather than for our own.

CHARLOTTE BRONTË

Frankly, I would take a cat over a cocktail party anytime.

CAROLYN G. HART

Certain flaws are necessary for the whole. It would

seem strange if old friends lacked certain quirks.

GOETHE

There is nothing better than the encouragement of a good friend.

KATHARINE BUTLER HATHAWAY

They're ultimately such mysterious little beings, and that's what I love about them. They do not disclose. They're very proud. If a cat falls off a table, it will right itself, start licking itself, and look over its shoulder at you as if to say, "Of course, I meant to do that."

ROSELLEN BROWN

A friend should be one in whose understanding and virtue we can equally confide, and whose opinion we can value at once for its justness and its sincerity.

ROBERT HALL

Truly it is a blessed thing to love on earth as we
hope to love in Heaven, and to begin that
friendship here which is to endure for ever there.

ST. FRANCIS DE SALES

*Friendship is neither a formality
nor a mode; it is rather a life.*

DAVID GRAYSON

*You are my only friend in the
world, and I want to talk to you.
Or, perhaps, be silent with you.*

G. K. CHESTERTON

Unlike us, cats never outgrow their delight in cat capacities,
nor do they settle finally for limitations.
Cats, I think, live out their lives fulfilling their expectations.

IRVING TOWNSEND

21

Certainly, cats have always recognized a kindred spirit in me. They're such beautiful creatures; they radiate such well-being and grace and relaxation that they always calm me down.

JILL KER CONWAY

It is a noble and great thing to cover the blemishes and to excuse the failings of a friend; to draw a curtain before his stains, and to display his perfections; to bury his weaknesses in silence, but to proclaim his virtues upon the housetop.

ROBERT SOUTH

A beloved friend does not fill one part of the soul, but, penetrating the whole, becomes connected with all feeling.

WILLIAM ELLERY CHANNING

A true friend embraces our objects as his own. We feel another mind bent on the same end, enjoying it, ensuring it, reflecting it, and delighting in our devotion to it.

WILLIAM ELLERY CHANNING

It's nice to have them around when I'm writing or reading, and it's very pleasant to have a companion.

ELIZABETH JANEWAY

What appeals to me is that strange combination of cozy, cuddly, you-can-tickle-their-tummies-and-they'll-lick-your-ear—and there's obviously something about them that's utterly remote from people, and I find that sort of nice.

EDWARD GOREY

24

Pure friendship inspires, cleanses,

*Friendship does not spring up
and grow great and become perfect
all at once, but requires time and
the nourishment of thoughts.*

DANTE

With the qualities of
cleanliness, affection,
patience, dignity, and
courage that cats have,
how many of us, I ask
you, would be capable
of becoming cats?

FERNAND MERY

expands, and strengthens the soul.

HORATIO ALGER

27

Friendly relations depend upon vicinity amongst other things,
and there are degrees; but the best kind of friendship
has a way of bridging time and space for all that.

H. R. HAWEIS

Friendship! the precious gold of life
By age refined, yet ever new;
Tried in the crucible of time
It always rings of service true.

Friendship! the beauteous soul of life
Which gladdens youth and strengthens age;
May it our hearts and lives entwine
Together on life's fleeting page.

AUTHOR UNKNOWN

A friend is he that loves, and he that is beloved.

THOMAS HOBBES

Friendship is a union of spirits,
a marriage of hearts, and the bond thereof virtue.

WILLIAM PENN

Sometimes I prefer cats; sometimes I prefer human company. It just depends on who the human is. Some cats are more cuddly than others, just like some humans.

KITTY KELLEY

I think cats deserve to live outdoors because they

really are miniature versions of lions and tigers.

JAY PARINI

It is a beautiful thing to feel
that our friends are God's
gifts to us. Thinking of it has
made me understand why we
love and are loved, sometimes
when we cannot explain
what causes the feeling.
Feeling so makes friendship
such a sacred, holy thing!

CICERO

Fellowship of souls
does not consist in the
proximity of persons.

Dr. Thomas

31

I simply can't resist a cat, particularly a purring one. They are the cleanest, cunningest, and most intelligent things I know, outside of the girl you love, of course.

MARK TWAIN

32